Pearls for the Soul

A Selection of Proverbs and Insights
Compiled by

RICHARD ALAN NAGGAR

Edited by

KATHLEEN MARIE BROWN

2010

Karen

You Are A lovely person
who brings warmth And
general Good feelings whenever
you Go. Now, Add these
"pearls" to your own
with Appreciation

Richard Moran

Page
8
#3

- Pearls for the Soul -
2010

.

The oyster creates a pearl over time. We forget about the rubbing, the friction and the pain of the process. We completely forget that the pearl came from a grain of sand that was an irritant to the oyster to begin with.

If you choose to believe it, even the oyster proclaims his glory.

- Richard Alan Naggar

The answer to one of the most profound questions is now upon you. This answer is complete; it is sufficient and it speaks with the authority that commands molecules and beyond, delivering a feather from a storm unharmed and intact, and causing a man to travel through infinity, yet live forever while doing it.

The answer? *I AM...tell them...I AM sent you...*

Now *you* must answer a profound question:

who are you? ...

... Who are you?

... Who are you?

*To the alpha and omega in us all
this work is dedicated.*

- *R.A.N.*

TABLE OF CONTENTS

PREFACE

Upon my introduction to *Pearls for the Soul*, I was immersed in them day and night. Some spoke to me personally with clear responses to questions which had arisen in my heart throughout my life. Others prompted me to delve beneath the surface of existence – into purpose, conscience, love and origins, where a deeper stratum of the soul was unearthed and heaved to the surface. Still, others began to mirror truth to me – truth about myself I had not previously seen: Who I am, who I'm not; what areas in me required more careful introspection, and what hidden things needed to be chased out by the light of truth. Throughout this process I've reflected, smiled, sorrowed, suffered and wept bitterly. The truth shall indeed set you free, but not before it has exposed you.

As answers began pouring in, I marveled that the home of all answers is the same source that prompts the questions in the first place...the same source who knows the end from the beginning and always finishes what it starts.

This book of *Pearls* has been a catalyst for what has become for me a wondrous adventure and the single most meaningful journey of my life.

- Kathleen Marie Brown

1

PREAMBLE

You are about to partake in some of the shared wisdom of your fellow man. Since the beginning of our time until now, these refreshments for the spirit have helped guide many on their journey.

You may be wondering why I've called them *Pearls for the Soul*. The soul is the essence, or core, of the human being – that place where God and man interact and understand each other through insight and revelation. The soul must be acknowledged, or fed, and if it is not, it eats what is available. Unfortunately, in today's environment, that diet consists mostly of earthly desires and treasures, which leave the soul hungry. We forget that the soul needs spiritual nourishment to thrive and grow. Feed the soul, and you have fed everything.

Look for the meanings behind the words, and let them move you to a deeper perspective on your life, your life's journey and your fellow man. The spirit in man will guide you there. Read slowly and randomly, letting something greater administer to your needs. You may laugh, cry, ponder and even repent, but I promise you will never be the same – nor will you want to be.

Prepare to recognize your place in eternity. Pearls for the Soul anyone? Bon voyage and bon appetit!

- Richard Alan Naggar

Note: Where "man" is mentioned, mankind is intended. Also, some of these words may sound familiar to you. Could it be that deep inside you are the seeds of these wisdoms? Revisiting these words may cause the seeds to grow. How much growth is up to the hearer and the doer. The origin of these words is more important than their authors, which is why they remain anonymous. Enjoy, and may you be touched deeply.

ADVERSITY

It's always sunny above the clouds.
·
Adversity is never pleasant, but sometimes it's possible to learn lessons from it that can be learned in no other way.
·
There is little adversity that cannot be conquered by a good plan implemented decisively.
·
A grain of sand adrift on the sea will still reach shore in spite of turbulent storms.
·
Many of us spend our whole lives running from our feelings, with the mistaken belief that we cannot bear the pain. But you have already borne the pain. What you have not done is explore beyond the pain.
·
When pain is sighted, victory is not far off.
·
One sees great things from the valley, only small things from the peak.
·
I was taught that the way of progress is neither swift nor easy.
·
We need to dwarf our troubles and magnify our blessings.
·
Anyone can hold the helm when the sea is calm.

When we long for life without difficulties, remind us that oaks grow strong in contrary winds, and diamonds are made under pressure.

·

The oyster creates a pearl over time. We forget about the rubbing, the friction and the pain of the process. We completely forget that the pearl came from a grain of sand that was an irritant to the oyster to begin with.

·

Good timber does not grow with ease. The stronger the wind, the stronger the trees.

·

Man cannot remake himself without suffering.

·

The course of true anything does not run smoothly.

·

Most of the important things in the world have been accomplished by people who have kept on trying when there seemed to be no hope at all.

·

The only antidote to mental suffering is physical pain.

·

The problem is not that there are problems. The problem is expecting otherwise and thinking that having problems is a problem.

·

Don't grieve. Anything you lose comes round in another form.

·

What doesn't kill me makes me stronger.

·

Pain is inevitable, suffering is optional.

·

Trouble is an opportunity in work clothes.

Drag your thoughts away from your troubles – by the ears, by the heels, or any other way you can manage it.
·

Tribulations we might have prevented through wise and honorable choices may finally teach us to become wise and honorable.
·

It is how you deal with failure that makes you a success.
·

True, stress can cause death, but when you meet it properly, you grow stronger – both in body and in spirit.
·

Your pain is the breaking of the shell that encloses your understanding. Even as the stone of the fruit must break so its heart may stand in the sun, so must you know pain.
·

Nothing is so bitter that a calm mind cannot find comfort in it.
·

I have sometimes been wildly, despairingly, acutely miserable, but through it all I still know quite certainly that just to be alive is a grand thing.
·

When in the midst of a challenge, be reminded that the pain is short-term and the pleasure of victory well worthwhile.
·

We must embrace pain and burn it as fuel for our journey.
·

In the middle of difficulty, lies opportunity.
·

Don't cry because it's over, smile because it happened.
·

Take away the complaint "I have been harmed," and the harm is taken away.

7

There is a time in the life of every problem when it is big enough to see, yet small enough to solve.

·

Great spirits have always encountered violent opposition from mediocre minds.

·

Our greatest glory consists not in never falling, but in rising every time we fall.

·

When you are sorrowful, look again in your heart, and you shall see that in truth you are weeping for that which has been your delight.

·

In the hour of adversity be not without hope, for crystal rain falls from black clouds.

·

The crisis of yesterday is the memory of tomorrow.

·

We turn to God for help when our foundations are shaking, only to learn that it is God who is shaking them.

·

No man may indeed become wise before he has had his share of winters in this world's kingdom.

Change & Growth

CHANGE & GROWTH

Mankind was not put here to fail.

•

My soul can find no staircase to heaven unless it starts
climbing now.

•

Home run hitters strike out a lot.

•

Go on working freely and furiously, and you will make
progress.

•

Try putting some legs on your next prayer.

•

Things don't change, but by and by our wishes change.

•

Every oak tree started out as a couple of nuts that stood
their ground.

•

If you always go with what you know, you'll never learn
and grow.

•

Satisfaction lies in the effort, not in the attainment.
Full effort is full victory.

•

We must all obey the great law of change...
it is the most powerful law of nature.

•

Put not off running toward, grasping or experiencing your
pain. Your growth awaits.

10

From the discontent of one man, the world's best progress springs.

•

Every blade of grass has its angel that bends over it and whispers, "Grow...grow and flourish."

•

The universe is full of magical things, patiently waiting for our wits to grow sharper.

•

Expect your every need to be met, expect the answer to every problem, expect abundance on every level, and expect to grow spiritually.

•

Seeing yourself as you want to be is the key to personal growth.

•

The universe is change; our life is what our thoughts make it.

•

Nothing endures but change.

•

Between stimulus and response is a space. In this space lies our freedom to choose our response. In these choices lie our growth and our happiness.
Let time guide you.

Character

CHARACTER

My riches consist not in the extent of my possessions, but in the fewness of my wants.

·

It is a blessed thing that in every age someone has had enough individuality and courage to stand by his own convictions.

·

Never does a man portray his character more vividly than his proclaiming the character of another.

·

You are what your deep driving desire is; as your deep driving desire is, so is your will; as your will is, so is your deed; as your deed is, so is your destiny.

·

One is never more on trial than in the moment of excessive good fortune.

·

Virtue is not left to stand alone. He who practices it will have neighbors.

·

Only he is successful in his business who makes that pursuit which affords him the highest pleasure, the thing that sustains him.

·

To gain that which is worth having, it may be necessary to lose everything else.

Your daily behavior reflects your deepest values.

·

Our deeds determine us as much as we determine our deeds.

·

It is impossible for a man to be cheated by anyone but himself.

·

Never give in to force or overwhelming odds. Hold to your convictions with honor and common sense.
Be patient! Then wait for your victory.

·

Money will come when you are doing the right thing.

·

Every man's work, whether it be literature or music or pictures or architecture or anything else, is always a portrait of himself.

·

He who gains victory over other men is strong; but he who gains victory over himself is all-powerful.

·

People, like nails, lose their effectiveness when they lose direction and begin to bend.

·

Conceal a flaw, and the world will imagine the worst.

·

The truth of the matter is that you ALWAYS know the right thing to do. The hard part is doing it.

·

It's not what a man has, but how he has come to have it.

·

What is popular is not always right, and what is right is not always popular.

Please all, and you will please none.

•

A pure intent opens the portals of the soul in such a way that only good can pass, but no evil can enter.

•

You may not be able to say what good is, but you will know when you have strayed from it by a pain in your soul that you feel as conscience.

•

Destiny is not a matter of chance, but of the inevitable consequences of our choices.

•

It is a man's lack of commitment to what is right – his lack of courage to resist what his selfish ego needs – that is the real problem.

•

There is never a better measure of who a person is than what he does when he is absolutely free to choose.

•

Nearly all men can stand adversity. But if you want to test a man's character, give him power.

•

The highest reward for a person's toil is not what he gets for it, but what he becomes by doing it.

•

Lacking principles does not stem from being weak, but being weak stems from lacking principles.

•

Pride always uses distraction as a means of escaping the keen observation of conscience.

•

There are times and situations in which it is extremely difficult to act; but then, that is the real test.

Such as are your habitual thoughts, such also will be the character of your mind; for the soul is dyed by the thoughts.

•

This is the last of human freedoms – to choose one's attitude in any given set of circumstances, to choose one's own way.

•

Character can be bought...at the cost of character.

Courage

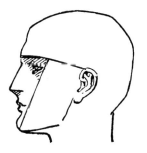

& Fear

COURAGE & FEAR

It is not because things are difficult that we do not dare; it
is because we do not dare that things are difficult.

•

The impossible is often the untried.

•

There is the risk you cannot afford to take, and there is the
risk you cannot afford *not* to take.

•

The coward dies a thousand deaths, the valiant only once.

•

Fall seven times, stand up eight.

•

Security is mostly a superstition. It does not exist in
nature, nor do the children of men as a whole experience it.
Avoiding danger is no safer in the long run than outright
exposure. Life is either a daring adventure or
nothing....SO GET MOVING!

•

Courage is like love; it must have hope for nourishment.

•

One man with courage is a majority.

•

A coward remains a coward until the next test of courage.

•

Leap, and the net will appear.

•

Everyone has a talent. What is rare is the courage to follow
the talent to the dark place where it leads.

With courage you will dare to take risks, have the strength
to be compassionate, and the wisdom to be humble.
Courage is the foundation of integrity.

•

Trust that still, small voice that says "This might work and
I'll try it."

•

Life shrinks and expands in proportion to one's courage.

•

Great deeds are usually wrought at great risk.

•

You must do the thing you think you cannot do.

•

The only way to pass any test is to take the test.

•

If you are not living on the edge, you take up too much
room.

•

Be as the little drummer boy who stood in line to play for
the King. No matter what grand gifts were given before
him, when it came to his turn, he gave the gift of all he had.
Never did the drum sound so sweet, and a king be so
pleased.

•

Fortune favors the bold.

•

Cowards die many times before their death.

•

When you try to do something you've never done before,
you risk falling on your face.

•

Everything in life is based on daring.

Daring ideas are like chessmen moved forward. They may be beaten, but they may start a winning game.

•

When your bow is broken and your last arrow spent, then shoot, shoot with your whole heart.

•

The mountain remains unmoved at seeming defeat by the mist.

•

Brave men are all vertebrates; they have their softness on the surface and their toughness in the middle.

•

Every man has his own courage, and is betrayed because he seeks in himself the courage of other persons.

•

Perfect valor consists in doing without witnesses that which we would be capable of doing before everyone.

•

Today, have courage for the great sorrows of life and patience for the small ones; and when you have laboriously accomplished your daily task, go to sleep in peace. God is awake.

•

Courage is resistance to fear, mastery of fear – not absence of fear. Except a creature be part coward, it is not a compliment to say it is brave.

•

We often give our enemies the means of our own destruction.

•

He said, "come to the edge." I said, "I can't." He said, "come to the edge." I said, "I can't - I'll fall off." He said finally, "come to the edge!" And I went to the edge, he pushed me, and then I flew!

Do not fear mistakes - there are none.

•

It is what we fear that happens to us.

•

Have you noticed that people threaten you with what they most fear?

•

Do the thing you are afraid to do, and the death of fear is certain.

•

It is not death that a man should fear, but he should fear never beginning to live.

•

A ship in harbor is safe, but that is not what ships are built for.

•

To him who is in fear, everything rustles.

•

Fear. I will tell you what to fear. Fear that you can walk by your fellow man, see his suffering, and not be moved by it. Fear that! Fear for your own soul.

•

Fear grows out of the things we think; it lives in our minds. Compassion grows out of the things we are, and lives in our hearts.

•

A good scare is worth more to a man than good advice.

•

Courage does not always roar. Sometimes courage is the small, quiet voice at the end of the day that says, "I will try again tomorrow."

Friendship

FRIENDSHIP

A friend is someone who reaches for your hand and touches your heart.

·

You can change your looks all you want, but I am your friend; you will still look the same to me.

·

Friendship improves happiness and abates misery by doubling our joys and dividing our grief.

·

The only reward of virtue is virtue; the only way to have a friend is to be one.

·

Celebrate the happiness that friends are always giving; make every day a holiday and celebrate just living.

·

Some people come into our lives and quickly go. Some people move our souls to dance. They awaken us to understanding with the passing whisper of wisdom. Some people make the sky more beautiful to gaze upon. They stay in our lives for awhile, leave footprints on our hearts, and we are never, ever the same.

·

When I look at the world I'm pessimistic, but when I look at people I am optimistic.

·

Nobody sees a flower, really, it is so small, it takes time. We haven't time, and to see takes time...like to have a friend takes time.

He who has a thousand friends has not a friend to spare, and he who has one enemy will meet him everywhere.

•

Of all the things which wisdom provides to make us entirely happy, much the greatest is the possession of friendship.

•

Don't walk in front of me, I may not follow. Don't walk behind me, I may not lead. Just walk beside me and be my friend forever.

•

A friend is someone who knows the song in your heart and can sing it back to you when you have forgotten the words.

•

A friendship is one soul living in two bodies.

•

To do someone a favor is a present. To have the person want to return the favor is a gift.

•

No man can be happy without a friend, nor be sure of his friend until he is unhappy.

•

Friendship is a very confusing part of life that makes a lot of sense.

•

In poverty and other misfortunes of life, true friends are a sure refuge. The young, they keep out of mischief; to the old they are a comfort and aid in their weakness, and those in the prime of life they incite to noble deeds.

Happiness

HAPPINESS

Happiness is like a butterfly which, when you pursue it, is always beyond your grasp, but which, when you sit down, may alight upon you.

•

That is happiness: to be dissolved into something complete and great.

•

If my heart can become pure and simple like that of a child, I think there probably can be no greater happiness than this.

•

Even if happiness forgets you a little bit, never completely forget about it.

•

You grow up the day you have your first real laugh at yourself.

•

A man who, as a physical being, is always turned toward the outside, thinking his happiness lies outside him, finally turns inward and discovers that the source is within him.

•

Fun has a sacred dimension.

•

Life is playfulness…we need to play so that we can rediscover the magical around us.

•

Laughter is the shortest distance between two people.

•

Success is simply defined as happiness.

More important than talent, strength or knowledge, is the ability to laugh at yourself and enjoy the pursuit of your dreams.

•

When you delight in the game, the effort seems unimportant.

•

Do not mistake happiness for the absence of misery.

•

Your day will go the way the corners of your mouth are turned.

•

There is no one luckier than he who thinks himself so.

•

A day without laughter is a day wasted.

•

You should sing like no one's listening, dance like no one's watching, love like you've never been hurt, and live like it's heaven on earth.

•

Happiness is not a goal; it is a by-product.

•

We learn the inner secret of happiness when we learn to direct our inner drives, our interests and our attention, to something outside ourselves.

•

Happiness is like jam. You can't spread even a little without getting some on yourself.

•

Oftentimes in denying yourself pleasure, you do but store the desire in the recesses of your being.

•

Happiness is not a station you arrive at, but a matter of traveling.

The foolish man seeks happiness in the distance; the wise man grows it under his feet.

·

Happiness sneaks through a door you didn't know you left open.

·

Remember this: very little is needed to make a happy life.

·

Peace comes from within. Do not seek it without.

·

Happiness is the harvest of a quiet eye.

·

If it's sanity you are after, there is no recipe like laughter.

·

The human race has one really effective weapon, and that is laughter.

·

Life is too important to take seriously.

·

The happy man is not he who seems thus to others, but who seems thus to himself.

·

If all our happiness is bound up entirely in our personal circumstances, it is difficult not to demand of life more than it has to give.

·

Most folks are about as happy as they make up their minds to be.

·

Man needs, for his happiness, not only the enjoyment of this or that, but hope and enterprise and change.

·

We are never so happy or unhappy as we think.

It is not easy to find happiness in ourselves, and it is not possible to find it elsewhere.

·

Humor is the affectionate communication of insight.

·

The greater part of happiness or misery depends on our dispositions, not our circumstances.

·

A smile is a curve that sets everything straight.

·

Three grand essentials to happiness in this life are something to do, something to love, and something to hope for.

·

If you never did, you should. These things are fun, and fun is good.

·

Different men seek after happiness in different ways and by different means, and so make for themselves different modes of life and forms of government.

·

Happiness depends upon ourselves.

·

Let us be grateful to people who make us happy; they are the charming gardeners who make our souls blossom.

·

Find ecstasy in life; the mere sense of living is joy enough.

·

We all live with the objective of being happy; our lives are all different and yet the same.

·

It is better to be happy for a moment and be burned up with beauty, than to live a long time and be bored all the while.

True happiness, we are told, consists in getting out of one's self, but the point is not only to get out of you, but to stay out; and to stay out, you must have some absorbing errand.

•

The highest happiness of man is to have probed what is knowable and to quietly revere what is unknowable.

•

You are forgiven for your happiness and your successes only if you generously consent to share them.

•

Happiness, that grand mistress of ceremonies in the dance of life, impels us through all its mazes and meanderings, but leads none of us by the same route.

•

Cheerfulness keeps up a kind of daylight in the mind, and fills it with a steady and perpetual serenity.

•

The really happy person is the one who can enjoy the scenery while on a detour.

•

Learn to smile, get the habit of it; learn to sing, make it also a habit, and you will be surprised how much brighter it makes the world – not only to others, but to yourself! The smile and the song lessen the burdens and light up the way.

•

Laugh yourself silly.

Kindness & Charity

KINDNESS & CHARITY

A man's true wealth is the good he does in the world.

·

There are those who give with joy, and that joy is their reward.

·

Be kind; for everyone you meet is fighting a harder battle.

·

The mark of a good action is that it appears inevitable in retrospect.

·

When negotiating with your neighbor, make sure he comes out well. In turn, he will be thinking the same of you.

·

How far that little candle throws his beams! So shines a good deed in a weary world.

·

Everyone can be great because everyone can serve.

·

The best way to knock the chip off your neighbor's shoulder is to pat him on the back.

·

It is one of the beautiful compensations of life that no man can sincerely try to help another without helping himself.

·

To receive everything, one must open one's hands and give.

·

Kindness is the noblest weapon to conquer with.

We cannot live only for ourselves. A thousand fibers connect us with our fellow men, and among those fibers, as sympathetic threads, our actions run as causes and come back to us as effects.

·

Once you have obtained sufficient food, shelter and clothing, turn your attention to your fellow man.

·

Kindness is more important than wisdom, and the recognition of this is the beginning of wisdom.

·

If you help others you will be helped, perhaps tomorrow, perhaps in one hundred years, but you will be helped. Nature must pay off the debt…it is a mathematical law and all life is mathematics.

·

You give but little when you give of your possessions. It is when you give of yourself that you truly give.

·

The more I give to thee, the more I have, for both are infinite.

·

Since you get more joy out of giving joy to others, you should put a good deal of thought into the happiness that you are able to give.

·

Regardless of others, be ever regardful of others.

·

You can never do a kindness too soon, for you will never know when it will be too late.

·

Tenderness and kindness are not signs of weakness and despair, but manifestations of strength and resolution.

Kind words can be short and easy to speak, but their echoes are truly endless.

·

Life is short and we have never too much time for gladdening the hearts of those who are traveling the dark journey with us. Oh, be swift to love, make haste to be kind, and be generous about it.

·

The course of human history is determined, not by what happens in the skies, but by what takes place in our hearts.

·

The greatest good you can do for another is not just to share your riches, but to reveal to him/her his/her own.

·

A word of encouragement during a failure is worth more than an hour of praise after success.

·

I don't know what your destiny will be, but one thing I do know: the only ones among you who will be really happy are those who have sought and found how to serve.

·

What makes the difference in life is not what is said, but *how* it is said.

Learn

Create

Imagine

LEARN, CREATE, IMAGINE

I would rather live in a world where my life is surrounded by mystery, than live in a world so small that my mind could comprehend it.

·

Real learning comes when the competitive spirit has ceased.

·

Never doubt that a small group of thoughtful, committed people can change the world. Indeed, it is the only thing that ever has.

·

When you know a thing, to hold that you know it – and when you do not know a thing, to allow that you do not know it – this is knowledge.

·

Memory is the greatest of artists, and effaces from your mind what is unnecessary.

·

All that we are is the result of what we have thought.

·

Goals that are not written down are just wishes. Wishes that are not lived out are dreams.

·

The man who succeeds above his fellows is the one who early in life clearly discerns his object, and towards that object habitually directs his powers.

·

Your life is dyed the color of your imagination.

There are many things I don't know, but there is nothing I can't learn!

·

The purpose of education is to replace an empty mind with an open one.

·

In the field of observation, chance favors the prepared mind.

·

Cut not the wings of your dreams, for they are the heartbeat and freedom of your soul.

·

If you think education is expensive, try ignorance.

·

In the beginner's mind there are many possibilities, but in the expert's mind there are few.

·

Learning is movement from moment to moment.

·

The "silly question" is the first intimation of some totally new development.

·

Nothing encourages creativity like the chance to fall flat on one's face.

·

Creativity is so delicate a flower that praise tends to make it bloom while discouragement often nips it at the bud.

·

Within our dreams and aspirations we find out it may be that those who do most, dream most opportunities.

·

Just as appetite comes by eating,
so work brings inspiration.

Imagination is more important than knowledge.

·

One learns by doing a thing; for though you think you know it, you have no certainty until you try.

·

Everywhere I go I find a poet has been there before me.

·

The capacity for delight is the gift of paying attention.

·

It is wise to have more questions than answers.

·

To do great work a man must be very idle as well as very industrious.

·

Learn to see, and then you'll know there is no end to the new worlds of our vision.

·

The more you know the less you understand.

·

A mind too active is no mind at all.

·

The world of reality has limits; the world of imagination is boundless.

·

The creative thinker is flexible and adaptable, and prepared to rearrange his thinking.

·

No great discovery was ever made without a bold guess.

·

Lack of money is no obstacle. Lack of an idea is.

·

Let the beauty we love be what we do.

·

Imagination is intelligence having fun.

He who wonders, discovers that this in itself is wonder.

•

Success is not the result of spontaneous combustion. You
must set yourself on fire.

•

The mind is not a vessel to be filled, but a fire to be
ignited.

•

Creativity can solve almost any problem. The creative act,
the defeat of habit by originality, overcomes everything.

•

I can't understand why people are frightened of new ideas.
I'm frightened of the old ones.

•

Imagination is a poor substitute for experience.

•

It is better to fail in originality than to succeed in imitation.

•

That which seems the height of absurdity in one generation
often becomes the height of wisdom in the next.

•

You don't understand anything until you learn it more than
one way.

•

Great minds have purposes, little minds have wishes.

•

Making mistakes simply means that you are learning faster.

•

The stories of childhood leave an indelible impression, and
their author always has a niche in the temple of memory
from which the image is never cast out to be thrown on the
rubbish heap of things that are outgrown and outlived.

•

What is now proved was once imagined.

Your dreams are as infinite and beautiful as the garden you plant them in.

•

The future belongs to those who believe in the beauty of their dreams.

•

If one advances confidently in the direction of his dreams, and endeavors to live the life which he has imagined, he will meet with a success unexpected in common hours.

•

How glorious it is – and also how painful – to be an exception.

•

Where all is but dream, reasoning and arguments are of no use, truth and knowledge nothing.

•

Some men see things as they are and ask "why?" But I dream things that never were and ask "why not?"

•

Dreams come true; without that possibility, nature would not incite us to have them.

•

It's time to start living the life you've imagined.

•

There comes a moment when you realize that virtually anything is possible – that nothing is too good to be true.

•

I never believed in trying to do anything. Whatever I set out to do, I found I had already accomplished.

•

Whatever you can do, or dream you can do, begin it.

•

Boldness has genius, power, and magic in it.

40

We are near waking when we dream we are dreaming.

·

Our dreams are the headlights with which we drive into the darkness of our future.

·

If you can imagine it, you can create it. If you can dream it, you can become it.

·

What we need is more people who specialize in the impossible.

·

Not all those who know their minds, know their hearts as well.

·

If you have built castles in the air, your work need not be lost; that is where they should be. Now, put the foundations under them.

·

But words are things, and a small drop of ink, falling like dew upon a thought, produces that which makes thousands, perhaps millions think.

·

All men dream, but not equally. Those who dream at night, by the dusty recesses of their minds, awake to find that it was vanity. But the dreamers of day are dangerous men – they that may act their dreams with open eyes to make them possible.

·

Magic has often been thought of as the art of making dreams come true, the art of realizing visions. Yet before we can bring birth to the vision, we have to see it.

·

There are no impossible dreams.

We teach what we live.

·

Your own words are the bricks and mortar of the dreams you want to realize. Your words are the greatest power you have. The words you choose, and their use, establish the life you experience.

·

A good answer is like a sweet kiss.

Life

LIFE

It's all about life being ahead of you, and you running at it.

•

In life, there are no accidents.

•

My father didn't tell me how to live; he lived, and let me watch him do it.

•

When you find you are an inspiration to others, then you have mastered life.

•

It is hard to swim against the flow of life.

•

Do not live life in the hope of becoming a memory.

•

Life is ours to be spent, not to be saved.

•

The question is not whether we will die, but how we will live.

•

To live is so startling it leaves little time for anything else.

•

There is no greater gift that any man can give, than to lay down his life for another. Count yourself worthy to receive it.

•

Life is not an exact science. It is an art.

•

Life is a mirror, what do you see?
You tell us, you tell me.

In the woods is perpetual youth.

•

For a long time it seemed to me that life was about to begin. My real life. But there was always some obstacle in the way, something to be gotten through first, some unfinished business; a debt to be paid, a place to go, and then my life would begin. At last it dawned on me that these obstacles were my life.

•

Live all you can; it's a mistake not to. It doesn't so much matter what you do in particular, so long as you have your life. If you haven't had that, what have you?

•

If there was one thing you would like to do before you die, or some place you would like to go, what would it be? Well?

•

A life spent making mistakes is not only more honorable, but also more useful than a life spent doing nothing at all.

•

Anyone who dies with one million dollars in the bank has missed the point.

•

If you can spend a perfectly useless afternoon in a perfectly useless manner, you have learned how to live.

•

In the long run, we get no more than we have been willing to risk giving.

•

To affect the quality of the day...that is the art of life.

•

I try to avoid looking forward or backward, and try to keep looking upward.

The meaning of life is to give life meaning.

•

The aim of life is to live, and to live means to be aware –
joyously, drunkenly, serenely, divinely aware.

•

The cost of a thing is the amount of what I call life, which
is required to be exchanged for it, immediately or in the
long run.

•

"I have done my best." That is about all the philosophy of
living one needs.

•

Live life as if you were granted three wishes and did not
need them at all.

•

Don't let your dreams interpret your life but rather your life
interpret your dreams.

•

Why do you grieve? Everything we have is on loan to us.
Use it wisely.

•

Life is a series of conquests. Water is a threat until you can
swim ... then it is a joy.

•

Each achievement develops increasing strength to conquer
greater stress.

•

Being on the tightrope is living; everything else is waiting.

•

When making your choice in life, do not neglect to live.

•

Dwell as near as possible to the channel in which your life
flows.

Life is a cup to be filled, not drained.

·

Life is not a spectacle or a feast; it is a predicament.

·

As long as you live, keep learning *how* to live.

·

If one is the master of one thing and understands one thing well, one has, at the same time, insight into, and understanding of, many things.

·

In three words I can sum up everything I've learned about life: it goes on.

·

Just because you are miserable doesn't mean you cannot enjoy life.

·

There are only two ways to live your life. One, as though nothing is a miracle; the other, as though everything is a miracle.

·

How we spend our days is, of course, how we spend our lives.

·

Health is the greatest gift, contentment the greatest wealth, faithfulness the best relationship.

·

The purpose of life is to live a life of purpose.

·

Everyone dies, but not everyone truly lives.

·

The whole life lies in the verb seeing.

·

May you live all the days of your life.

In the game of life there is nothing to lose except by not playing.

•

Purpose serves as a principle around which to organize our lives.

•

When you were born, you cried and the world rejoiced; live your life so that when you die, the world cries and you rejoice.

•

When we were born, school of life started; when we die, school is out.

Love

LOVE

The highest form of love a man can have is the need to
merge his soul with God.

·

The true test of love is what one is willing to do for others.

·

Love washes away from the soul the dust of everyday life.

·

A man should offer his wife a new kind of security. It is
the security of her knowing that he is loyal for love's sake,
good for goodness sake, and not just a bee after the honey.

·

Love is to risk friendship by telling the truth because you
care about one's soul.

·

Hearts will break and yet brokenly they live on.

·

True love is innocent and free, no strings attached.
It gives and goes merrily on its way.

·

There are never enough "I love yous."

·

Love is the beauty of the soul.

·

We may never know what love is,
but we know what it isn't.

·

If you love life, life will love you back.

·

The happiness of love is in action.

The love we seek comes more from loving others than from being loved.

•

If I could reach up and hold onto a star for each time you've made me smile, I'd have the entire night's sky in the palm of my hand.

•

What matters most, if I may boast about the things we share, is nothing much, but to feel your touch, and know you're really there.

•

One of the best feelings in the world is to love, admire, and respect someone who you know loves, admires, and respects you just as much.

•

To regard another's health, wealth, welfare, happiness, feelings, needs, and aspirations equal to or above your own, is to love them.

•

I don't love you because I need you; I need you because I love you.

•

I have yet to find the words to express how I feel; while he has yet to find the feelings expressed by such words.

•

Love is but a gift of sharing your heart with another and being willing to accept part of theirs.

•

To see the love YOU feel in someone ELSE'S eyes is the greatest happiness.

•

Pains of love be sweeter far
than all the other pleasures are.

Too many of us stay walled because we are afraid of getting hurt. We are afraid to care too much for fear that the other person doesn't care at all.

·

I don't make you feel special; I just remind you that you are special!

·

In the passing of time, I knew not the true value of love until my love was taken for granted.

·

A man who was married for 50 years to his beloved, was asked at her funeral if there was something more he could have done for her. He responded with tears, "yes, I could have loved her more."

·

Treasure each other in the recognition that we don't know how long we shall have each other.

·

Maybe God wants us to meet a few wrong persons before meeting the right one so that when we meet the right one, we should know to be grateful for the gift!

·

In love, as in war, a fortress that parleys is half taken.

·

A job is what we do for money; work is what we do for love.

·

It is only with the heart that one can see rightly; what is essential is invisible to the eye.

·

A loving person lives in a loving world. A hostile person lives in a hostile world: everyone you meet is your mirror.

·

We are shaped and fashioned by what we love.

Life is a journey, and love is what makes that journey worthwhile.

•

The best and most beautiful things in this world cannot be seen or even heard, but must be felt with the heart.

•

The heart is wiser than the intellect.

•

A smile is a light in the window of the soul indicating that the heart is home.

•

To the world you may be one person, but to one person you may be the world.

•

If we want a love message to be heard, it has to be sent out. To keep a lamp burning, we have to keep putting oil in it.

•

Never apologize for showing feeling. When you do so, you apologize for the truth.

•

The mind has a thousand eyes, and the heart but one; yet the light of a whole life dies when love is done.

•

Love gives naught but itself and takes naught but from itself. Loves possesses not, nor would it be possessed; for love is sufficient unto love.

•

Hell is the only place outside of heaven where we can be safe from the dangers of love.

•

Hate is love looking for itself everyplace but where love is.

•

If a thing loves, it is infinite.

You cannot really love someone who never makes you laugh.

•

It is better to have loved and lost than to never have loved at all.

•

Relish love in your old age! Aged love is like aged wine...it becomes more satisfying, more refreshing, more valuable, more appreciated and more intoxicating!

•

But to see her was to love her, love but her, and love forever.

•

Oh, thou art fairer than the evening air clad in the beauty of a thousand stars.

•

I am my beloved's, and my beloved is mine.

•

We loved with a love that was more than love.

•

Love knows not its own depth until the hour of separation.

•

In bed, my real love has always been the sleep that rescued me by allowing me to dream.

•

The greatest happiness of life is the conviction that we are loved – loved for ourselves, or rather, loved in spite of ourselves.

•

This is the true measure of love: When we believe that we alone can love, that no one ever could have loved so before us, and that no one will ever love in the same way after us.

Mankind writes because it is driven by the need to communicate. Behind the need to communicate is the need to share. Behind the need to share is the need to be understood. Behind the need to be understood is the need to be wanted. Behind the need to be wanted is the need to be loved. Write this down: love one another.

•

Oh, what a recreation it is to be in love! It sets the heart aching so delicately; there's no taking a wink of sleep for the pleasure or the pain.

•

Grow old with me! The best is yet to be.

•

Is not absence death to those who love?

•

The only reaching of man's heart is through love, which is the middle ground of discretion. It neither attacks nor defends, but makes others ashamed by its nobility, virtue and patience; and above all, by its complete indifference in response to antagonism and temptation.

•

In dreams and in love there are no impossibilities.

Nature

NATURE

The spider's touch, how exquisitely fine! Feels at each thread, and lives along the line.

•

There is pleasure in the pathless woods, there is rapture in the lonely shore, there is society where none intrudes, by the deep sea, and music in its roar; I love not Man the less, but Nature more.

•

The spectacle of the sky overwhelms me. I'm overwhelmed when I see in an immense sky, the crescent of the moon, or the sun and stars.

•

The veins of a maple leaf, like the paths of life, travel in all directions.

•

There are moments in most days when I feel a deep and sincere gratitude, when I sit at the open window and there is a blue sky or moving clouds or light rain.

•

Muddy water when still, becomes clear.

•

At the head of every river lies a spring.

•

God gave us a memory so that we could have roses in December.

•

What the caterpillar calls the end of the world the master calls a butterfly.

You can complain because roses have thorns or you can rejoice because thorns have roses.

•

All art is but imitation of nature.

•

The love of nature is consolation against failure.

•

How does the bee know how to build the honeycomb? How does the bird know how to build its nest? What about the geese...that they know when to fly south for the winter? As with all living things, it is inside of us, and if only we would listen to it, oh, what harmony. Oh, what a world it would be!

•

Half the failures in this world arise from pulling in the reins on one's horse while it is leaping.

•

I died and became a mineral; then, the mineral fed a plant; then, the plant fed an animal; then, the animal was consumed by a man; then, that man died. Why should I fear? When was I less by dying?

•

Do not follow where the path leads, rather go where there is no path, and leave a trail.

•

Give light, and the darkness will disappear of itself.

•

Keep sowing your seed, for you never know which will grow.

•

If anything is sacred, the human body is sacred.

•

Adopt the pace of nature.

I would rather be ashes than dust; I would rather that my spark should burn out in a brilliant blaze than it should be stifled by dry-rot; I would rather be in a superb meteor, every atom of me in magnificent glow than in a sleepy and permanent planet; the proper function of man is to live, not to exist; I shall not waste my days in trying to prolong them; I shall USE my time.

•

You see the Earth as a bright blue and white Christmas tree ornament in the black sky. It's so small and so fragile – you realize that on that small spot is everything that means anything to you; all of history and art and death and birth and love. The big picture is just fine.

•

To measure you by your smallest deed is to reckon the ocean by the frailty of its foam. To judge you by your failures is to cast blame upon the seasons for their inconsistencies.

•

If you see a whole thing, it seems it's always beautiful. Planets, lives...but up close, a world's all dirt and rocks.

•

A blade of grass is no less than the journey-work of the stars.

•

If you just set people in motion they'll heal themselves.

•

All of the animals except man know that the principal business of life is to enjoy it.

•

Man is a make-believe animal – he is never so truly himself as when he is acting a part.

We live in a rainbow of chaos.

•

Nature never lies.

•

The moment one gives close attention to anything, even a blade of grass, it becomes a mysterious, awesome, indescribably magnificent world in itself.

•

To keep the body in good health is a duty...otherwise we shall not be able to keep our minds strong and clear.

•

I want to sing like the birds sing, not worrying about who hears or what they think.

•

Rest is not idleness, and to lie sometimes on the grass under trees on a summer's day, listening to the murmur of the water or watching the clouds float across the sky, is by no means a waste of time.

•

Try to pluck a thistle and plant a flower wherever the flower will grow.

•

If you take a flower in your hand and really look at it, it's your world for the moment.

•

Your body is precious. It is your vehicle for awakening. Treat it with care.

•

The way I see it, if you want the rainbow, you gotta put up with the rain.

•

Until he extends his circle of compassion to include all living things, man will not himself find peace.

Flowers feed the soul.

•

To see a world in a grain of sand, and heaven in a wild flower, holds infinity in the palm of your hand, and eternity in an hour.

•

If one cannot collect all the beautiful shells on the beach, what then?

•

Beauty, more than bitterness, makes the heart break.

•

Every man has a rainy corner of his life whence comes foul weather, which follows him.

•

When you look up at the sky, you have a feeling of unity, which delights you and makes you giddy.

•

Nature does nothing uselessly.

•

And the day came when the risk to remain tight in a bud was more painful than the risk it took to blossom. The first flower was then born.

•

Hold fast to dreams, for if dreams die, life is a broken winged bird that cannot fly.

•

Who says the eternal being does not exist?
Who says the sun has gone out? Someone who climbs up on the roof, closes his eyes tight and says, "I don't see anything," is fooling himself.

•

Hurt not the earth.

You are a child of the Universe, no less than the moon and the stars; you have a right to be here. And whether or not it is clear to you, no doubt the Universe is unfolding as it should.

·

What if you slept; and what if in your sleep you dreamed; and what if in your dream you went to heaven and there you plucked a strange and beautiful flower; and what if when you awoke you had the flower in your hand? Oh, what then? What then?

Perspectives

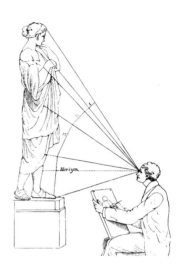

PERSPECTIVES

Let God be God and man be man.

•

We don't see things as they are, we see them as *we* are.

•

In heaven, an angel is nobody in particular.

•

The man who says I can and the man who says I can't are both right.

•

Hope is the poor man's bread.

•

There is nothing either good or bad but thinking makes it so.

•

If you train hard you'll not only be hard, but you'll be hard to beat.

•

Lend everyone your ear, but not your mouth.

•

The man who has no inner life is a slave to his surroundings.

•

Water which is too pure has no fish.

•

It is better to deserve an honor and not receive it, than to receive one, and not deserve it!

•

The best remedy for anger is delay.

•

Every exit is an entry somewhere else.

Anger blows out the lamp of the mind.

•

There is a great deal of unmapped country within us which would have to be taken into account in explanation of our gusts and storms.

•

The body may come and go, but the soul, like God, is deathless.

•

He who knows enough is enough will always have enough.

•

Home is not where you live but where you are understood.

•

There is only one blasphemy, and that is the refusal to experience life.

•

Every exit is an entry somewhere else.

•

Ah, but a man's reach should exceed his grasp, or what's heaven for?

•

The tendency of an event to occur varies inversely with one's preparation for it.

•

Keep away from people who try to belittle your ambitions. Small people always do that, but the really great make you become great.

•

Everyone takes the limits of his own vision for the limits of the world.

•

It is not good to be too free. It is not good to have everything one wants.

Staying in the moment and watching without judgment makes hell go away. No evil can stand to be observed by the light of innocence.

·

If you were able to face the world calmly, without resentment, nothing could move you off center or threaten your self-respect.

·

Every luxury must be paid for, and everything is a luxury, starting with being in the world.

·

Nothing is sadder than the death of an illusion.

·

Energy creates energy. It is by spending oneself that one becomes rich.

·

The reward of a thing well done is to have done it.

·

People deal too much with the negative...with what is wrong. Why not try and see positive things, to just touch those things and make them bloom?

·

If the only prayer you said in your whole life was "thank you," and meant it, that would suffice.

·

If I have seen farther than others, it is because I was standing on the shoulders of giants.

·

I would rather fail in a cause that will ultimately triumph than to triumph in a cause that will ultimately fail.

·

Everything has beauty, but not everyone sees it.

Fortune is like glass – the brighter the glitter, the more easily broken.

•

Beware lest you lose the substance by grasping at the shadow.

•

The man who makes no mistakes does not usually make anything.

•

Success is never final, but failure can be.

•

What is right is often forgotten by what is convenient.

•

Only those who do nothing make no mistakes.

•

There is no failure, only feedback.

•

Failure is the opportunity to begin again, only more wisely.

•

I have not failed 10,000 times, but I have found 10,000 ways that do not work.

•

When one door closes, another opens. Life stops when you do.

•

You cannot teach a crab to walk straight.

•

A great city is not to be confounded with a populous one.

•

There is no more miserable human being than one in whom nothing is habitual but indecision.

•

Luxury is more deadly than any foe.

What we obtain too cheaply, we esteem too little;
it is dearness only that gives everything its value.

•

The value of gold is what it is because of what it takes to
go get it.

•

Battle not with monsters, lest you become a monster, then
gaze into the abyss and the abyss gazes into you.

•

Certain defects in people may be necessary for the
existence of individual.

•

The saints are the sinners that just keep going.

•

The reason why worry kills more people than work is
because people worry more than they work.

•

Of all the sad words of tongue and pen,
the saddest are these: It might have been.

•

A man can do all things if he but wills them.

•

Half the work that is done in the world is to make things
appear what they are not.

•

Because I am a woman, I have to make unusual efforts to
succeed. If I fail, no one will say, "She doesn't have what
it takes," they will say, "Women don't have what it takes."

•

People are like stained glass windows; they sparkle and
shine when the sun is out, but when the darkness sets in,
their true beauty is revealed only if there is a light from
within.

Pursue what you love, and you'll never work a day in your life.
·

If that which is below us influences us more than that which is above us, then that which is around us will control that which is within us.
·

We can live a life by choice or by chance.
By chance we taste nothing. By choice we savor everything.
·

If you "do nothing" right, you will do nothing wrong.
·

It is not what you tell your self, but what your self tells you.
·

How many cares one loses when one decides not to be something, but to be someone.
·

The highest is not to understand the highest, but to act upon it.
·

If you take care of the small things, the big things take care of themselves. You can gain more control over your life by paying closer attention to the little things.
·

Sometimes holding on makes you stronger; sometimes it's letting go.
·

Man is not free to refuse to do the thing which gives him more pleasure than any other conceivable action.
·

The best way out is through.
·

Success is never final.

It is extraordinary how extraordinary the ordinary person is.

·

The soul should always stand ajar, ready to welcome the ecstatic experience.

·

It is eternity now. I am in the midst of it.
It is about me and the moment.

·

The reason angels can fly is that they take themselves so lightly.

·

The fundamental delusion of humanity is to suppose that I am here and you are out there.

·

Don't ever save anything for a special occasion. Being alive is a special occasion.

·

There is nothing either good or bad, but thinking makes it so.

·

Doubt is a thief.

·

The sorrow which has no vent in tears may make other organs weep.

·

If the doors of perception were cleansed, everything would appear to man as it is: Infinite.

·

Move your hand, blink your eye or take a breath and you have participated in eternity.

·

Less is more, more or less.

It has long been an axiom of mine that the little things are infinitely the more important.

•

It has been my experience that folks who have no vices have very few virtues.

•

Freedom is nothing else but a chance to be better.

•

There are two ways of spreading light; to be the candle or the mirror that reflects it.

•

One can never consent to creep when one feels an impulse to soar.

•

Once we make our decision, all things will come to us. Auspicious signs are not a superstition, but a confirmation. They are a response.

•

The Universe awaits your next choice.

•

Until one is committed, there is hesitancy, the chance to draw back, always ineffectiveness. Concerning all acts of initiative (and creation), there is one elementary truth, the ignorance of which kills countless ideas and splendid plans: Inaction. At the moment one definitely commits oneself, then Providence moves too. All sorts of things occur to help one that would never otherwise have occurred. A whole stream of events issues from the decision, raising in one's favor all manner of unforeseen incidents and meetings and material assistance, which no man could have dreamt would have come his way.
Take Action!

If you think you are too small to be effective, you have never been in bed with a flea.

•

Luck is when opportunity knocks and you answer.

•

Can it be that each of us are angels with only one wing; and we can only fly by embracing one another? Should we not fly high?

•

Things which matter most must never be at the mercy of things which matter least.

•

Remember and never forget that you pass this way once, never to return.

•

There is only one way to come into this world; there are too many ways to leave it.

•

Do the math:
You come with nothing. You die with nothing.
What have you lost? Nothing!

•

We were not sent into this world to do anything into which we cannot put our heart.

•

An age is called Dark, not because the light fails to shine, but because people refuse to see it.

•

The most important things are the hardest to say, because words diminish them.

•

Such as we are made of, such we be.

Words are, of course, the most powerful drug used by mankind.

•

Each small task of everyday is part of the total harmony of the universe.

•

Look at everything as though you were seeing it either for the first or last time. Then your time on earth will have more meaning.

•

A cathedral, a wave of storm, a dancer's leap, never turn out to be as high as we had hoped.

•

You'll never know how far you might have progressed until you commit to step past the point of no return.

•

In the end, we all get what we deserve.

Seek

Journey

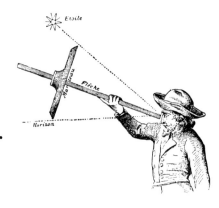

Discover

SEEK, JOURNEY, DISCOVER

Let go and let's go!
·
The beginning is the most important part of the work.
·
The journey begins when you look down at your feet and command them to go.
·
One of the noblest inquiries one can make is to question the meaning of life. It is your motive for asking, which will trigger the response.
·
A good traveler has no fixed plans and is not intent on arriving.
·
Wheresoever you go, go with all your heart.
·
Still, around the corner there may wait a new road or a secret gate.
·
It is good to have an end to journey toward, but it is the journey that matters in the end.
·
Do not seek to follow the footsteps of the men of old. Seek what they sought.
·
To be surprised, to wonder, is to begin to understand.

Go confidently in the direction of your dreams! Live the life you've imagined. As you simplify your life, the laws of the universe will be simpler.

·

Putting one foot in front of the other only begins the journey. Everything else you need to know will come after you start.

·

Though we travel the world over to find the beautiful, we must carry it with us or we would find it not.

·

Even if you are on the right track, you will get run over if you just sit there.

·

The only joy in the world is to begin.

·

There are many things in life that will catch your eye, but only a few will catch your heart. Pursue those!

·

No man can reveal to you ought but that which is already inside of you waiting to awaken.

·

When the student is ready, the master appears. To ready the master, the student appears.

·

People only see what they are prepared to see.
Once you become objective to the grandiose delusions of your earthly mind you will be subjective to the heavenly mind.

·

One doesn't discover new lands without consenting to lose sight of the shore for a very long time.

We pray for simplicity, we get clutter. We pray for harmony, we get discord. We pray for opportunity, we get difficulty. Why then do we complain when our prayers are always being heard and answered?

·

Don't wait for moods. You accomplish nothing if you do that. Your mind needs to know it has to get down to work.

·

The journey of a thousand leagues begins from beneath your feet.

·

The answer is simple. If you want something very badly, you may have it.

·

Look and you will find it – what is unsought will go undetected.

·

Life is a promise; fulfill it.

·

Twenty years from now you will be more disappointed by the things you didn't do than by the ones you did. So throw off the bowlines. Sail away from the safe harbor. Catch the trade winds in your sails. Explore. Dream. Discover.

·

Every step of the journey is the journey.

·

Even if all our efforts of attention seem for years to be producing no result, one day a light that is in exact proportion to them will flood the soul.

I do not know what I may appear to the world; but to myself I seem to have been only like a child playing on the seashore, and diverting myself now and then, finding a smoother pebble or a prettier shell than ordinary, whilst the great ocean of truth lay all undiscovered before me.

·

The soul looketh steadily forward, creating a new world before her, leaving worlds behind her.

·

Chance is always powerful. Let your hook be always cast; in the pool where you least expect it, there will be fish.

·

Listening to what conscience is trying to tell us about our problems is the beginning of truly listening to God.

·

The voyage of discovery is not in seeking new landscapes but in having new eyes.

·

There are things that are known, and things that are unknown. In between there are doors.

·

Remember to have faith; to believe without seeing.

·

The feeling remains that God is on the journey too.

S E L F

W H O A M I ?

SELF - WHO AM I ?

To be nobody but myself in a world which is doing its best, night and day, to make me someone else, means to fight the hardest battle any human can fight, and never stop fighting.

·

In order to experience oneself, one must experience the world entire.

·

Develop an interest in life as you see it; the people, things, literature, music – the world is so rich, simply throbbing with rich treasures, beautiful souls and interesting people. Forget yourself.

·

There is only one of you in all time. This expression is unique, and if you block it, it will never exist through any other medium, and it will be lost.

·

When you are feeling depreciated, angry and drained, it is a sign that other people are not open to your energy.

·

Ask yourself: What did I bring to the party? Everything was here when I arrived. Therefore, what is required of me?

·

You're on! It's your turn. You're on!

·

Mirrors point out the faults you see in yourself when you look at others.

Make the most of yourself – that's all there is to you.

·

Think highly of yourself because the world takes you at your own estimate.

·

Learn to understand first and to be understood second.

·

If you work hard on your job you will make a living. If you work hard on yourself you will make a fortune!

·

Everyone is unique. Compare not yourself with anyone else, lest you spoil God's curriculum.

·

Put your heart, mind, intellect and soul into even your smallest acts. This is the secret of success and quality of life.

·

Beware how you take away hope from any human being.

·

Self-pity in its early stages is as snug as a feather mattress. Only when it hardens does it become uncomfortable.

·

I do not wish to be everything to everyone, but I do wish to be something to someone.

·

Count yourself lucky if you can count yourself.

·

You've got to find the force inside you.

·

Try. What is that? Do or do not...there is no try.

·

It is better to be trusted than to be loved.

Trust in yourself. Your perceptions are often more accurate than you are willing to believe.

·

The human body is naturally lazy; only your mind can pick it up and drive it.

·

When you start to doubt yourself, the real world will eat you alive.

·

Your work is to discover your work and then with all your heart, give yourself to it.

·

"More has been done with less." This means that even though you may have a limited supply of something (love, hope, courage, or whatever) don't let it stop you, you gotta work with the cards you were given and play your hand.

·

Nobody can give you wiser advice than yourself.

·

The most terrifying thing is to accept oneself completely.

·

To know what you prefer instead of humbly saying 'Amen' to what the world says you ought to prefer, is to have kept your soul alive.

·

You haven't failed till you quit trying.

·

Stop thinking and talking about it and there is nothing you will not be able to know.

·

Saying "no" can be the ultimate self-care.

Let me listen to me and not to them.

·

I need to take an emotional breath, step back and remind myself who's actually in charge of my life.

·

There is luxury in self-reproach. When we blame ourselves, we feel no one else has a right to blame us.

·

Let yourself be open and life will be easier. A spoon of salt in a glass of water makes the water undrinkable. A spoon of salt in a lake is almost unnoticed.

·

When we cannot find contentment in ourselves, it is useless to seek it elsewhere.

·

To love oneself is the beginning of a life-long romance.

·

Hell begins the day God grants you the vision to see all you could have done, should have done, and would have done, but did not do.

·

Beauty is eternity gazing at itself in a mirror. But you are eternity and you are the mirror.

·

Ask questions whenever you are not sure, but always make your own choices.

·

We do not believe in ourselves until someone reveals that deep inside us something is valuable, worth listening to, worthy of our trust, sacred to our touch. Once we believe in ourselves we can risk curiosity, wonder, spontaneous delight or any experience that reveals the human spirit.

What lies behind us and what lies before us are tiny matters compared to what lies within us.

·

To believe your own thought, to believe that which is true for you in your private heart is true for all men, that is genius.

·

Compassion for myself is the most powerful healer of them all.

·

Always dream and shoot higher than you know how to. Don't bother just to be better than your contemporaries or predecessors. Try to be better than yourself.

·

You can search throughout the entire universe for someone who is more deserving of your love and affection than you are yourself, and that person is not to be found anywhere. You, yourself, as much as anybody in the entire universe, deserve your love and affection.

·

The only way you can truly love and respect yourself, is to be what you truly love and respect.

·

We cannot be who we need to be unless we change who we are.

·

Have faith in yourself; refuse to believe in the word "impossible." Only you know what you want and need.

·

Your aspirations are your possibilities.

·

Carry the law for your behavior within yourself.

Let the pain and the pleasure both be yours, and learn to recognize the voices.

•

Be careful what you set your heart on, for it will surely be yours.

•

From time to time, to remind ourselves to relax, to be peaceful, we may wish to set aside some time for a retreat, a day of mindfulness, when we walk slowly, smile, drink tea with a friend, and enjoy being together as if we are the happiest people on earth.

•

Remember, no one can make you feel inferior without your consent.

•

The greatest compliment that was ever paid me was when someone asked me what I thought and attended to my answer.

•

Whenever you find yourself on the side of the majority, it's time to pause and reflect.

•

A person must turn and face himself in order to understand himself.

•

Your conscience knows everything you know, and it knows that you know it!

Stillness

& Solitude

STILLNESS & SOLITUDE

To sit quietly and think is the hardest thing a person can do,
for when he does, all the demons of the universe show up
and try to keep him from the truth. But these demons must
be faced, then slain, in order to live a life worth living.

•

Do not rely completely on any other human beings.
We meet all life's greatest tests alone.

•

It is better to remain quiet and be thought a fool than to
speak up and remove all doubt.

•

No great work has ever been produced except after a long
interval of still and musing meditation.

•

Our life is frittered away by details. Simplify…Simplify
and Simplify!

•

True silence is rest of the mind; it is to the spirit what sleep
is to the body – nourishment and refreshment.

•

Teach us to care and not to care. Teach us to sit still.

•

If you are seeking creative ideas, go out walking.
Be still. Listen. Angels whisper to a man when
he goes for a walk.

Solitude is the furnace of transformation.

·

If you keep your mouth shut, you will never put your foot in it.

·

In your heart, keep one still, secret spot where dreams may go and take shelter, so they may thrive and grow.

·

The quieter you become the more you can hear.

·

Most men live lives of quiet desperation.

·

Only when one is connected to one's inner core is one connected to others. For me, the core, the inner spring, can best be re-found through solitude.

·

I was never less alone than while by myself.

·

To be at peace with ourselves we need to know ourselves.

·

If there is to be any peace it will come through being, not having.

·

How beautiful it is to do nothing, and then rest afterward.

·

Sit quietly, doing nothing, spring comes and the grass grows by itself.

·

It takes a lot of time to be a genius – you have to sit around so much doing nothing, really doing nothing.

·

An intellectual improvement arises from leisure.

One of the lessons of history is that nothing is often a good thing to do and always a clever thing to say.

·

The good and the wise lead quiet lives.

·

You must learn to be still in the midst of activity and to be alive in your silence.

·

No trumpets sound when the important decisions of our life are made. Destiny is made known in a silent way.

·

There are chapters in every life which are seldom read, and certainly not aloud.

·

Being still and doing nothing are two completely different things.

·

Become as little children.

TIME

and Patience

TIME & PATIENCE

You will never find time for anything. You must make it.

·

Time is but the stream I go a-fishin' in. I drink at it, but while I drink I see the sandy bottom and detect how shallow it is. Its thin current slides away, but eternity remains.

·

If you wait for tomorrow, it comes. If you don't wait for tomorrow, it comes.

·

It takes less time to do a thing right, than it does to explain why you did it wrong.

·

You can discover more about a person in an hour of play than in a year of conversation.

·

Time you enjoyed wasting is not wasted time.

·

What we do today, right now, will have an accumulated effect on all our tomorrows.

·

Slow down and enjoy life. It's not only the scenery you miss by going too fast - you also miss the sense of where you are going and why.

·

Do it now before another moment passes.

When we get too caught up in the busyness of the world we lose connection with one another and ourselves.

•

We do not remember days, we remember moments.

•

Be intent upon the perfection of the present day.

•

Live in the moment. If you dwell on the past or focus on the future, you'll miss what is wonderful today.

•

The best thing about the future is that it only comes one day at a time.

•

Live for today. Yesterday is gone and tomorrow may not come.

•

You only live once – but if you work it right, once is enough.

•

She who loves roses must be patient and not cry out when she is pierced by thorns.

•

Life is but a moment, death also is but another.

•

No eternal reward will forgive us now for wasting the dawn.

•

The years teach much that the days never knew.

•

If you build up too many tomorrows, all you end up with are a bunch of empty yesterdays.

92

The timeless in you is aware of life's timelessness, and knows that yesterday is but today's memory and tomorrow is today's dream.

•

Procrastination is the art of keeping up with yesterday.

•

So much of our time is preparation; so much is routine, and so much retrospect, that the path of each man's genius contracts itself to a very few hours.

•

It is wise and respectful to give thought to all those that have gone before you. Upon their deaths, the baton of life was handed to you. Run a good race and live a good life, then pass the baton.

•

Let us rise up and be thankful, for if we didn't learn a lot today, at least we learned a little, and if we didn't learn a little, at least we didn't get sick, and if we got sick, at least we didn't die; so, let us all be thankful.

•

Punctuality is the thief of time.

•

Patience is the key to paradise.

•

Life is not a matter of milestones, but of moments.

•

You can't change the past, and you can ruin a perfectly good present by worrying about the future.

•

Look at your watch and count back ten seconds, or look at your watch and count forward ten seconds, or live those seconds. The choice is yours.

The future you shall know when it has come; before then, forget it.

•

I must govern the clock, not be governed by it.

•

Today I live in the quiet, joyous expectation of good.

•

What would be the use of immortality to a person who cannot use well a half an hour?

•

The world is moving so fast these days that the man who says it can't be done is generally interrupted by someone doing it.

•

Time will explain it all. Time is a talker, and needs no questioning before he speaks.

•

Dost thou love life? Then do not squander time, for that is the stuff life is made of.

•

Life's tragedy is that we get old too soon and wise too late.

•

Manhood a struggle; old age a regret.

•

The days that are still to come are the wisest witnesses.

•

However gradual the course of history, there must always be the day, even an hour and minute, when some significant action is performed for the first or last time.

•

If you don't have time to do it right, you must have time to do it over.

We can do anything we want as we stick to it long enough.

·

Patience is the companion of wisdom.

·

The person who removes a mountain begins by carrying away small stones.

·

It takes a long time to bring excellence to maturity.

·

Through perseverance many people win a success out of what seemed destined to be certain failure.

·

Never Never Never Never give up!

·

Life is so short and we must learn to move very slowly.

·

The key to everything is patience. You get the chicken out of the egg by hatching it and not by smashing it.

·

What you pursue, you don't get. But what you allow to grow slowly in its own way, comes to you.

·

Just as impatience is the primitive energy of pride, so is patience the "force" behind humility.

·

Time is a unique teacher. He gives the test and then teaches the lesson.

·

Patience acquires itself in patience.

·

"The moment" is that ambiguity in which time and eternity touch each other.

Truth

& Wisdom

TRUTH & WISDOM

To perceive the truth about evil is the first step toward
being saved from its power.

•

Trust in reality, for in it is hidden the gate to eternity.

•

Willingness to believe the truth is to live the truth.

•

Truth is not in words, but in the understanding of their
meaning.

•

The truth does not bind or control by any form of
compulsive response. You can change the outward
"motion" of people by force, but never their inner motive.

•

Don't respond to life. Respond instead to the principle that
is the meaning of life. Respond to the still unchanging
nature of truth.

•

Wisdom is not in words. Wisdom is meaning within
words.

•

Wisdom begins with wonder.

•

Belief consists in accepting the affirmations of the soul;
unbelief, in denying them.

Meditation brings you back to the present moment, to the now, where the truth lives always, where we can experience His presence, where He can take our sins upon Himself and give us back our bright nature to bond with His purity.

•

We know how to speak many falsehoods that resemble real things, but we'll know, when we will, how to speak true things too.

•

Wise men make proverbs, but fools repeat them.

•

If you cannot find the truth right where you are, where else do you expect to find it?

•

Long years must pass before the truths we have made for ourselves become our very flesh.

•

Intense feelings too often obscure truth.

•

The least initial deviation from truth is multiplied later a thousandfold.

•

The first key to wisdom is steadily attentive, frequent questioning.

•

By three methods we may learn wisdom: First, by reflection, which is noblest; second, by imitation, which is easiest; and third by experience, which is bitterest.

•

When practicing wisdom, be quick to overlook.

•

Religion is merely the law which binds man to the creator.

We pray for courage, then danger comes so that courage might be. We ask for wisdom, but receive trouble, so that wisdom might come. We pray for love, but receive torment, so that love will reply. Why is it that we complain then, that our prayers are not being heard and answered?

•

If you can bear humiliation without resenting it, it will turn into humility, and humility will lead to salvation.

•

Sit down before truth as a little child, be prepared to give up every conceived notion, follow humbly wherever and whatever abysses nature leads you into, or you will learn nothing.

•

All great truths begin as blasphemies.

•

The soul is a room that is never vacant. If good does not live there, evil does, and that is the pure and simple truth.

•

The best is yet to be.

•

A good book has no ending.